How to write your first book.

→||← Made skinny.
Fast & Easy to read.

By Tony Sharples

Copyright © 2024 by Antony John Sharples.

All rights reserved.

No part of this book may be reproduced, stored in a retrieval system, or transmitted in any form or by any means, electronic, mechanical, photocopying, recording, or otherwise, without the prior written permission of the Copyright owner.

Contact: sharples.writer@gmail.com

ISBN 978-1-7636554-3-0

Although the author and publisher have made every effort to ensure that the information in this book was correct at press time, the author and publisher do not assume and hereby disclaim any liability to any party for any loss, damage, or disruption caused by errors or omissions, whether such errors or omissions result from negligence, accident, or any other cause.

Contents

Dedication	V
1. Why This Skinny Book Format?	1
2. The Journey That Lead To My First Book.	3
3. Choose Your Mountain.	8
4. How To Climb Your Writer's Mountain.	11
5. Don't Get Discouraged.	26
6. Choosing Which Mountain To Climb.	27
7. Write Your First Book To Learn How To Write A Book.	30
8. You need to get writing. Now!	35
9. Mistake #1 Not Finding Your Creative Time And Space.	37
10. Mistake #2 Writing Your First Book With A Complex Storyline.	47
11. Mistake #3 Shooting For Perfection.	51
12. Mistake #4 Not Understanding Editing and Formatting Before You Write.	55
13. Mistake #5 Thinking About Publishing Too Late In Your Process.	66

14. Mistake #6   74
Not Understanding The Economics.

15. Mistake #7   82
Thinking Getting Feedback Will Be Easy.

16. Mistake #8   84
Not Allowing Time And Money For Marketing.

17. Mistake #9   87
Not Setting Some Hard Deadlines.

18. Stop Calling Yourself An Author.   91
19. What should you do next?   92
20. A Real World Example.   95
21. Please Leave A Review.   99

I'd like to dedicate this book to my sister, Julie.
Having self-published several books, she's been
an invaluable source of advice for my first book and also for this one.
My first two books would not exist without her.

I

Why This Skinny Book Format?

This is a skinny book compared to most.

I kept it tight so you could read it fast.

It's short on pages but long on useful information for first-time authors.

It's not a definitive guide to writing, publishing and distribution. If you want to do a deep-dive on those topics, there are millions of chunky books out there. By doing some simple searches, you can find brilliant advice from expert YouTube channels. Beyond that, you'll find plenty of writing courses and writer groups that cover the tradecraft of writing a book perfectly. Presenting you with more of the same information would be a complete waste of your time. So, I won't do that.

Instead, this book will focus on the crucial mistakes you can make when writing your first book. Uncluttered. In as few words as possible.

When you see this symbol, I've added some insights and specific examples from my experience writing my first book (Weed War).

Online resources are available.

I haven't crammed this book with detailed information about how I went about writing my first book. Every time I did that, the book just got thicker. I also didn't want to put a lot of specific details in the book because they can go out of date.

For example, right now I couldn't say enough good things about Atticus as a tool for formatting my books. They recently did a major update to add some collaboration features to it which wrecked a lot of its functionality. Times change.

I've shifted a lot of the specific elements to a dedicated section on my author's website (www.tonysharples.com), so I can make updates at any time.

In that part of the website you'll find specific details on the software I use, many of the processes that I followed for my first book, plus some guides to self-publishing, marketing and the business of book writing. I'll also include links to interesting feeds, podcasts and blogs that might be helpful.

You can go to the site by clicking on the QR code on the back cover of the book. Or just use the one below.

2

THE JOURNEY THAT LEAD TO MY FIRST BOOK.

I've done a lot of writing, but only just started my journey as an author.

This book is based on my recent experiences of finishing my first book and getting it out into the marketplace.

It's a summary of the things I wish I'd known back when I started.

I'll tell you upfront, I'm not an industry expert. I don't come from a publishing background. My experience comes from being a writer in the world of advertising and marketing.

In my professional career, I developed many advertising campaigns for brands like Coca-Cola, Pepsi, Heineken, Volkswagen, IBM and many other global brands. I've worked in countries stretching from Egypt to Australia, and most places in between.

I've written TV commercials with multi-million-dollar budgets featuring global music and movie stars. I've also done my fair share of writing long-form copy for things like press releases, HR manuals, websites, PowerPoint decks and brochures. The not-so-glamourous work of the corporate world.

Early in my career, I studied writing and production. I wrote several screenplays and scripts for TV series. I studied screen-craft and writing at UCLA and did multiple film production courses. I've spent more days standing around on film sets watching cameras roll than I care to remember.

When I hit my early thirties, it was crunch-time. I had to make a big decision. Was I going to be a writer? Or something else?

Like a poker player, I had to decide whether I was going to go "all-in" on a youthful writing career or was I going to "fold".

I folded.

I gave up writing and dived deep into the world of global marketing.

It paid fabulously. I traveled the world shooting TV commercials, got to fly in private jets, and hung out with lots of celebrities. I once got to travel in a presidential motorcade. It was a good choice, in my mind.

Advertising taught me about story structure and writing. I worked on every stage of most campaigns from the original idea, through the production process and then the release of the ad campaign into the market. I did everything from creating epic Pepsi TV commercials to writing copy for long and often boring HR staff induction tools.

Advertising taught me about writing, but it's nothing like the literary world.

Creating advertising is about telling interesting stories, but it's not art. Everything you do operates on strict deadlines. Time matters. The work you do has to lead to a result, in terms of product sold or perceptions changed. You complete a project, then quickly move to the next one.

As I progressed in the world of advertising, that forgotten writing career always nagged at me.

One day, I would come back to it. One day, I would write my epic dream book.

My Dream Book.

Just like you, I had an inkling I could be good at writing a book.

I had an idea for an epic novel burning a hole in my brain. A story set in the goldfields of the mid-1800s, about rugged Australian bushrangers and desperate highway robberies.

I did all my research and worked out the plot structure. I'd watched Sorkin videos on writing and motivations, read many books on storytelling and taught myself how to use Scrivener as a writing tool.

I was ready to go, but there was one problem.

I didn't know how to write a book. I'd never done it before.

Time to write.

I finally found time in my schedule to try writing a book.

I was excited. My first step was to research and map out the potential storyline for my epic bushranger story.

It was then that I hit a fork in the road.

I realised there was a steep learning curve ahead of me, so I had two choices:

First, I could stop writing; and spend a lot of time studying the art of writing, publishing, and selling a book. Then start my epic story again.

Second, I could continue writing; and learn everything during the process of writing my epic story. Learn-as-you-go.

After grappling with these two options, I decided there was actually a third way of doing it.

I did what I came to call, *"Writing a book, to learn how to write a book."*

Rather than sit down and spend the next two years writing an epic tome about bushrangers, I took a writing tangent for six months, writing a short, simple book that would actually TEACH me how to write.

This led to my first published fiction novel called Weed War. It's an adventure book, with a military flavour.

It's the book I wrote to learn how to write a book.
I set myself a hard deadline of six months to get it completely finished.
Take no prisoners. More about this in Chapter 16.

Paying it forward.

This book passes on what I learned during the process of writing my first book.

My motivation for writing it is to pay it forward for other people about to start the same journey. Take out of it what you want and discard the rest.

Which of these two mountains would you find easiest to climb?

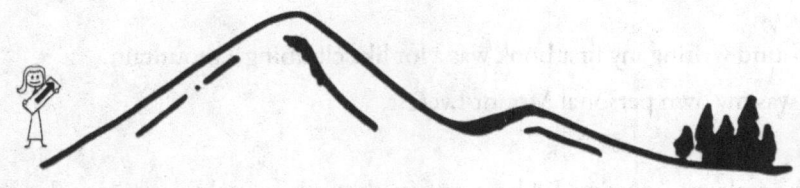

3

CHOOSE YOUR MOUNTAIN.

I found writing my first book was a lot like climbing a mountain.
It was my own personal Mount Everest.

The scale was massive. I'd have to pass through several base-camps along the way. I'd reach forks on the track where I had to decide the best way to go.
Worst of all, I'd have to learn how to mountain-climb as I struggled my way towards the summit.
To me, it seemed doomed to fail.

I decided on a change of plan.
Rather than trying to climb Mount Everest straight away, I instead climbed a smaller mountain first.

My first book, Weed War, was that smaller mountain.
I'd learn my mountain climbing skills on it, then I'd tackle Everest.

What's ahead?

In the next chapter, we'll run through the process of writing, publishing, and marketing your first book.

I'll be using a mountain climbing analogy to make it simple.

In the chapters after that, we'll look at the nine specific mistakes first-time authors, like you and I, tend to make .

4

How To Climb Your Writer's Mountain.

'It is not the mountain we conquer, but ourselves.'
Sir Edmund Hillary.

Thousands of people have climbed Mount Everest over the years.

They all have two things in common: First, they have a burning desire to get to the summit. Second, they have amazing mountaineering skills.

Nobody just turns up at the bottom of the mountain, like a tourist on a day trip, and decides, 'hey, I'm going to climb that today.'

Climbing the mountain takes planning.

At Everest, you'll start on flat ground at Base-Camp, at the foot of the Kumbhu Icefall. Nice and easy. At 6,000 metres you'll reach Camp 1, where you'll stop for a while to a acclimatise. Just above that sits Camp 2, where you'll rest and prepare for the rest of the climb. The climb turns difficult after Camp 3 on the Lohtse Face. This is where you will start to use ropes to scale the steep and dangerous ice slopes. The final Camp sits at 8000 metres. It's called the South Col. From here, you'll make your push to the summit.

To echo the words of Sir Edmund Hillary, you'll need to pass a series of physical and mental camps on your journey to write and publish your first book. You'll come close to giving up at some of the hardest stages, but when you reach the summit, you'll be holding the first copy of your book in your hands. Feeling on top of the world.

Base-Camp: Before you climb.

Your journey up your writers mountain will start on flat ground.

Before you take any steps uphill, you will have practiced and honed your skills. You might have already done a course, read many books or joined a writer's group to boost your skills.

At Base-Camp, you'll get all your gear together and create your plan for the climb.

You'll map out your storyline, characters and their arcs of discovery. Maybe you'll talk to other writers to get feedback on how they structured their books they've written, or you'll do lots of reading in similar genres.

Some of you will decide to take a path that's less planned. A writer who is a "pantser" might prefer to set out for the summit with no fixed climbing path in mind, but they are still heading for the summit.

***

My experience at Base Camp was incredibly messy.

As I prepared to write, I ended up with stacks of paper all over the room, with notes blue-tacked to the wall. I had folders on Google Drive stuffed with reference notes. Every few weeks, I discovered new ways to streamline the process, but most of the time, it just added to the mess.

One thing I learned early was that there is plenty of software out there to help you at this first stage. I was creating a lot of Google Docs, but still drowning in paper and notes. Then I discovered Scrivener.

Learning Scrivener was incredibly complex and frustrating. I gave up on it twice, reverting to the simplicity of Word and Google. Eventually I was able to master it.

All I can say is that, if your book has a relatively complex story and cast of characters, tools like Scrivener will help you greatly. The major benefit is that having everything on the screen in front of you allows a quick return to the story when you begin a new writing session. It's also great if you want to reshuffle the chapters and move things around.

Don't get me wrong, Word can do exactly the same, but the price you pay for simplicity is that it's less efficient,

The big advantage to me was having all the information readily available on the screen, allowing for a quick return to the story when starting a new writing session. You can see your reference and notes in a click rather than having to fossick through paperwork or computer folders.

***

At the base of the writer's mountain, your primary objective is to get your shit together.

Now it's time to hit your keyboard, and do the climb to the first Camp.

Camp 1.

You'll reach Camp 1 when you've completed the first draft of your manuscript.

For the sake of brevity, this book won't dwell on the skills required to write your manuscript. There are plenty of brilliant books and courses on that already.

In the chapters ahead, we'll focus on your writing process.

***

When I started writing my first book, I was totally fixated on finishing the first draft. Nose down, tail up, in front of the computer screen.

I was only looking at the journey to Camp 1. While pumping words into the keyboard, I was totally focused on things like story, pace, arcs, and character development.

However, the Climb to Camp 1 was only a small part of the journey to the summit. There were still plenty of camps to be navigated.

Looking back, I wish I'd spent a bit more time in the early days learning about the camps further up the mountain. I should have given more thought to things like editing, formatting, my publishing options, the sales channels, profitability and marketing. Not to become an expert, but just to understand where they fit into the writing process.

I should have taken off a few days and spent more time watching YouTube videos, listening to writing and publishing podcasts, and reading books about the industry. Looking back, it would have made my process of writing my first draft much easier. There was so much that I didn't know. You can find free information on how I used software like Plottr, Word, Scrivener and Atticus at my author's website.

***

You'll be ready to depart for Camp 2 when you feel happy to show what you've written to others.

Camp 2.

This camp is where you'll tackle the editing and formatting of your first draft.

The terrain ahead is going to get steeper and tougher. It will be less familiar as you step in to the unfamiliar world of editing and formatting.

There's an entire chapter ahead that talks about editing and formatting.

***

My personal experience was that I found the editing and formatting process to be massively more complex, and painful, than I originally thought it would be.

Good editors are expensive, so you need to factor in that cost, and the time it will take to get someone to do the editing for you. It isn't a quick process.

If you can't afford professional editing, you can always do it yourself. You can use friends and family as your editing team. It's cheap, but it has some downsides. We will talk about this later in the book, too.

After I finished my first draft, my editing process was predominantly driven by time. I was working to a really strict deadline and didn't think I had the time to get external editors involved. Looking back, that was probably a mistake, but was one I was prepared to live with in order to meet my deadlines.

Dumb things got in the way, too.

Manually printing out multiple paper copies of the book to give to people to read wasn't really practical. The first draft was well over 400 pages. So I gave friends and family readers PDF or .doc files instead. Then I discovered that those types of files are terrible to read unless you are looking at them on a computer screen. They just don't work well on phones and mobile devices. The perfect solution would have been to give them an e-book version, but I didn't know how to create that type of format of the book back then.

I naively thought this part of the writing process was going to take a couple of weeks. It ended up taking several months. I've been told it takes traditional publishers up to three years to take a new manuscript through this process because it has to pass through so many sets of hands along the way.

I found this part of the writing process incredibly frustrating. I learned to hate my manuscript during this part of the journey.

Thankfully, I fell back in love with it during the climb to the next camp.

Don't forget you can find more specific and updated information on editing and formatting for books, ebooks and audiobooks at my author's website.

Just like writing your first draft, you will eventually reach a point where you are happy to say the magic words, 'This is ready to publish'.

Camp 3. Publishing your physical, e-book and audiobook.

If a traditional publisher picks you up, it's a bit like being joined by a team of sherpas and climbing experts at this camp. They will do a lot of the work to get you to the summit. Woo Hoo!

If you choose the self-publishing path, there will be unexpected twists and turns to navigate during this part of the climb. You'll reach many forks where you'll have to make important decisions about which direction you will travel.

As you reach those forks on the climbing path, you'll make decisions that will determine your path to the top of the mountain. Some people will be happy to just do a paperback and never do an e-book version. Others will want to splurge and do premium hardcover versions as well. The choice to step into the domain of audiobooks is for the brave (or those who can throw cash at it).

When publishing my first book, I made many discoveries.

I decided to self publish because I wanted to get the whole project finished as quickly as possible. My sister had done some self-publishing before, so she could provide a good sounding board for this part of the process.

As I grappled with the publishing process, the main things I learned were:

- Publishing a novel is fairly straightforward because it's really just a cover image wrapped around a printed PDF file.

- Image-based books, like cookbooks and children's picture books, are far more complex because they involve things like typography and artwork. The software tools are complex.

- Outputting an e-book version can be simple if you use the right software. It can be a nightmare if you don't know what you're doing or don't really understand how e-books are technically different from printed books.

- Creating an audiobook version adds a whole new level of complexity.

As with the earlier parts of the journey up the mountain, dumb things got in the way. I battled for a couple of weeks trying to format my book for publishing using Scrivener. That was the dumbest thing ever. It was like trying to dig a large hole with a fork.

More about this is coming up in a chapter ahead.

During this part of the climb, I also encountered a monster called "design".

The design of your cover, and the blurb you put on it, are critical to the success of your book, both in stores and online. It's not about looking attractive or striking. Your cover needs to stand out next to other books on a bookstore shelf, but it equally needs to look good as a postage stamp sized image on an online bookstore you are looking at, using on a phone or tablet. Like most good design, it's part art and part science.

These are never straightforward decisions to make. You'll have to learn how to evaluate what "works" and what doesn't. You don't want to risk doing all that hard work to write the book, then edit and format it, only to have it look like crap on the shelf or in an online store.

My main learning about the design aspect of publishing is to not leave it until too late in the overall process. I didn't really start thinking about it until I was very close to pushing the button to publish the book.

As with editing, many writers choose to use outside experts to create their book covers for them. There are lots of great freelance people out there who can do a great job for you. If down that path, you need to make an allowance for the time and money that will require.

***

Your completion of this section of the climb will deliver one of the most enjoyable parts of the entire journey up the mountain.

There's nothing quite like the feeling you get when you hold the first proofed copy of your book, in your hands or on a Kindle screen. It's pure magic.

But you are still a long way from the top of the mountain!

Now you have an actual book, and it's available for sale. You are ready to set off for the next camp.

You can find more specific and updated information on my use of services like Thorpe Bowker and Ingram Spark at my author's website.

Camp 4. Setting your sales and profit strategy.

There's never been a better time to sell books.

The online platforms and distribution options are incredible. My first book, which I published through Ingram Spark, is available on the behemoths like Apple and Amazon, but I've also seen it in many obscure little online bookstores in places like Japan, Indonesia and Norway.

Once again, I wish I'd spent more time researching what I could reasonably sell my book for and what the resulting profit per book would be. It might have influenced the genre and category of book I choose to write, and maybe the audience I aimed for with my story.

We'll talk more about this in Chapter 12. Of course, you can also find more specific and updated information at my author's website.

A reality check.

Once your book is available, your pricing strategy is critical. There are some realities you need to be aware of if you are going to maximise the chances of your first book being a sales success.

- Your biggest potential sales market is likely to be America.

- A sizeable portion of those sales will be eBooks (which many people will read in black and white on Kindles, or on iPads).

- The most popular genre is trashy holiday reads (saucy romance stories, sci-fi, etc). That's where the honey pot of money lives.

- The self-help and education arenas are incredibly busy and competitive. Soon, AI might significantly harm this sector of the market. More on this Chapter 7.

- Your ability to make a reasonable income from your first book is akin to being discovered waiting tables in Hollywood and becoming a famous actor. It's possible, but unlikely.

- Many times, particularly in self-publishing, you will have little control over the ultimate selling price of your book in the online stores.

Are you in it for money or love?

As soon as I started writing, I made a commitment to expanding my knowledge of the book market by watching videos, taking part in online forums and listening to author and publisher podcasts.

What I've seen has been eye opening, to say the least. When it comes to sales and profits, book writing can be a fairly irrational business.

I'm constantly gob-smacked when I read online publishing forums. I see a slew of stories about authors who've worked hard to write a brilliant book but really don't understand how to make a liveable income from it.

What's more surprising is that many of them don't seem to consider what their sales and profits strategies are going to be BEFORE they start writing. They just seem to assume that if the writing is good enough, it will find them an audience and give them a viable income stream.

There's an entire chapter ahead that looks at the economics of book writing.

You need to think about money matters early in the writing journey, so you don't end up writing a book that will have a very hard time reaching its market or making a buck.

If you're mostly writing for passion, this isn't so much of a concern.

If you're ultimately writing to help pay your bills, it is.

Once you've set an acceptable income strategy for the book, you're ready to head for the next camp.

Getting people to buy it.

Camp 5. Marketing your book.

Congratulations. You've reached the stage where your book is available for sale, at a price and profit margin you're happy to live with. Now you need to get people to buy copies of it.

If you get picked up by a traditional publisher, this part of the process will be relatively easy for you because they will throw a team of experienced marketing people at it.

If you go down the self-publishing path, you will find parts of the marketing process mind-boggling. There's a simple reason for that. It's highly unlikely that you are a book marketing expert, so you are going to have to study hard to learn how to do it.

Chances are, you aren't a marketing whiz.

I was lucky. I'd spent most of my professional career creating advertising strategies and campaigns for brands with millions of dollars to spend. I still found marketing of my own book very difficult.

That's because the oldest adage in marketing still rings true.

> 'Half the money I spend on advertising is wasted. The trouble is I don't know which half.' – John Wanamaker, A famous ad exec.

Most new authors I see online talk about how much it costs and what a crap-shoot it is. They've tried Facebook ads, TikTok videos, YouTube, Amazon Ads, Google AdWords, email newsletters, ARC (Advance Review Copies), campaigns to build reviews, book touring events and a million other marketing options.

Trying to do just one of these options is hard. Trying to do all of them well is nigh on impossible. Don't forget you can find more specific and updated information about book marketing at my author's website.

I had to make some hard decisions when I reach this stage because I faced a classic "Catch-22" situation.

Time vs Money.

You can pour time, money and effort into the marketing of your first book, but the problem is that it's the ONLY book you have. If I reader buys it and likes it, you have nothing else available to sell them. That's incredibly limiting for a new author.

Many experienced authors will tell you the most efficient marketing approach is to wait until you have, maybe, three books published and available for sale before you start any sort of serious marketing.

That created a problem for me. The more time I spent marketing my first book, the less time had to write my second and third books. Catch-22.

This is one of the most difficult things I've had to juggle on my writing journey.

I desperately want to spend more time marketing my first book, but every minute I'm doing that I'm not sitting in front of a screen writing the books that follow it.

After lots of soul searching, I bit the bullet and decided that my priority would be to get more books out, rather than focusing on the marketing of the first one. That could wait. I wanted to start writing again.

One essential.

I spent some time building a simple author's website. I thought it would be important to allow people to find out more about me and the books I was writing.

The site expands the amount of blurb people can read about the book. It also lets me give them the opportunity to read some examples of the writing in the book and it lets me have a simple way to capture people's email addresses if they are interested.

I have a QR code that links to the website, so I can use it on different marketing materials. The QR code also appears on the back cover of the book.

***

Once your marketing strategy is in place, you've really reached the end of the process of writing your first book.

What's next?

The Summit.

The view from the summit differed from what I was expecting.

I was expecting a feeling of completion. Satisfied that my book was out there in the wild. I'd just turn my focus to writing my next book. Onwards and upwards!

As time went by, I discovered books are like plants or pets. They require constant nurturing and care. Every minute I'm tending to my first book means I'm not busy writing my second and third. That first book always seemed to demand my attention.

My dilemma.

I'd love to do an audiobook version of my first book. I've also read that, in my home market, it's one of the most profitable sales avenues available. So it makes sense to do it, on multiple levels.

The problem is that creating an audiobook would be a huge amount of work. Significantly more than creating the original printed and ebook versions. I used Atticus to format the pages, and it made creating those two versions incredibly easy.

So, standing at the top of the mountain, I faced a dilemma.

Do I spend my time going through the complex process of creating an audiobook or do I spend time writing my second book (which is really my original dream book).

I finally decided on a different path, which I'll talk about in Chapter Six.

5

DON'T GET DISCOURAGED.

I was listening to a podcast yesterday where they were talking to a group of successful authors about how they started writing.

They asked them that classic question; 'If you could pass on one piece of advice to the person you were when you started writing, what would it be?'

One writer made an interesting comment. She said she wouldn't pass any advice or knowledge back because she was worried that it would have discouraged her and she never would have started. Her biggest learning over the years was that the process of writing the first drafts of your books is actually just a small part of the overall task every author faces.

I agree with her, but the good news is the overall process gets easier and easier the more times you do it. I've just written and self-published my second book (this book) and it was massively easier than the first one. I realised that I have learned so much along the way. So keep that in mind. It gets easier and easier. My third book will be the large and complex bushranger story I've always wanted to write. I'm now about ninety pages into the first draft of that book, and the lessons from the first two books are making the overall process much easier.

That's why, as I'm going to suggest in the next two chapters, it's a good idea for you to taste the experience of writing, publishing, distributing and marketing a book as early as possible in your writing career.

6

Choosing Which Mountain To Climb.

You've just discovered that writing, publishing and marketing your first book is a bit like climbing Mount Everest.

But there are many sizes and types of mountains out there. Some of them are steep and dangerous. Others are like a Sunday walk in the park.

Like you, most new writers wouldn't choose to climb Mount Everest as their first book writing project. No training. No practice. No skills. It makes sense to choose something smaller and simpler, then build your way up.

Before trying to climb a gigantic mountain, you would:

- Do a lot of pre-planning. You'd think about things like the weather and the route you'd take.

- For months before the climb, you'd build your fitness and your climbing skills.

- You'd make sure you have the correct tools for each part of the climb. And you'd definitely make sure you know how to use them.

You'd climb smaller, easier mountains first to get some practice before you tackle the big one. Your approach to writing should be the same as that.

Which type of mountain is best for your first attempt?

Surprisingly, this isn't what many writers do when tackling their first book. New authors tend to just turn up at the bottom of the hill and start walking up.

They start with an idea burning inside them. A killer cookbook. An epic murder-mystery. An amazing life story. Then they map out the flow of the story. They look at other books to get a broad understanding of how the fundamentals if writing a manuscript work. Some might do a course or join a writing group.
Then they sit down at a computer and start writing.
Chapter 1. Let's go!

The other day I was listening to a podcast where an editor was talking about a client who'd just finished a 100,000 word manuscript. The writing was great, but the author was having an incredibly difficult time writing a 200 word blurb summary of the story. It wasn't something that he ever considered he'd have to do. At the end of the process, one of his lessons was that he really wished he'd done a version of that simple 200 word summary before he began. It would have set a clearer direction for the hundred thousand words he was about to write.

For most writers, like you, the first book you will be burning to write is your "dream story". It's your big kahuna. The idea that's been gnawing away inside your gut. Desperate to get out. That big kahuna deserves to get the very best shot you can give it. The aim of this book is to help you give it the best shot.

How to give your dream book the best shot.
You need to think about how you should approach writing your first book. The key word here is "approach".

I'd like to convince you that writing your thick, epic dream book isn't the best option for your very first book.

A better approach might be to climb a small mountain first, to build the skills you'll need to do a great job climbing the big one. Don't start by writing your dream book. Get match-fit as a writer first.

I like to call this *"writing a book to learn how to write a book."*

7

WRITE YOUR FIRST BOOK TO LEARN HOW TO WRITE A BOOK.

When I started writing, I decided not to write my epic bushranger book first.

I wanted to give my big kahuna the best shot possible. I wasn't a skilled writer and knew little about the book market. Little money was available for luxuries like paid developmental editing during the writing of my first draft.

I didn't want to risk screwing that story up by learning-on-the-go. I wrote a shorter, simpler story first.

I explained to friends I was "writing a book to learn how to write a book."

This would let me put a toe in the publishing water by doing a small, simple publishing project, from end to end. I'd climb a small mountain first. From ground to summit.

I'd use that first book to make sure I was match-fit to write the books that would follow.

How can you follow this approach?

- Write a short book on a topic that is very familiar to you.

- Give it a short, hard deadline to complete.

- Don't worry if it's not perfect. You're writing this book to learn how to write a book. It isn't a literary masterpiece. It's alright if it's just the best you can do in a limited period.

- Give birth to the book in the easiest way possible. Self-publish it in both physical and digital formats. Consider doing a no-frills audio version.

- Conduct some simple marketing to familiarize yourself with the options out there. Don't spend a lot of time or money on it.

- Don't spend too much time, money or effort on things like professional editors, beta readers, ARC, professional cover art, online advertising, etc. Your primary focus should be to get the book through the entire writing, publishing and marketing processes quickly as possible.

- Don't be a perfectionist. Make lots of mistakes, over a very short period, and learn from every one of them.

Then, with all of this wonderful experience under your belt, you really will be match-fit as a writer. Now you are ready to move on to writing your original masterpiece.

***

Once I had climbed my small mountain, I saw the book-world through fresh eyes. I'd completed the writing and publishing process from end-to-end.

In a short period, I'd made many mistakes I wouldn't be repeating.

My writing had become more seasoned, and I was in a far better position to interact with the industry (either traditional agents or self-publishing) when my manuscript was done.

***

What if you can't get match-fit by climbing a small mountain first?

Don't worry if you can't allocate the time or effort to write a book to learn how to write a book. If you're already too deep into your epic story, I'd suggest a couple of options you could consider.

First, you could just pause your current project.

Climb a ridiculously small mountain, by writing a ridiculously small book.

Last time I looked, the minimum book size on the IngramSpark self-publishing platform was just eighteen pages.

Consider taking a hiatus from your current project. Just two or three weeks.

Spend it by writing a short book. Maybe fifty pages. Once again, basing it on a topic that you will find really easy and natural to write about. Treat it like a long-ish short story. Maybe a novella.

You will need to set hard dates for writing, editing, formatting, publishing, making available for distribution plus some token marketing once it gets online.

If you use a writing tool like Atticus, it will do most of the formatting and preparation for publishing for you as you write. It will also give you a simple means to push out an e-book version so you can get experience of publishing that way.

Join the Atticus Authors Facebook group so you can experience the type of conversations that authors are having already about the writing and publishing process.

Many new authors use freelance creative services like Fiverr to get their cover designs and blurb done at a very low cost.

Note: many writers think self-publishing a book like this will tarnish them in the eyes of the traditional publishing trade. Nothing could be further than the truth. Yes, it's a given that you can write a great story to start with. But equally they are looking for authors who they can work with easily. If you have a good helicopter-view of how writing, publishing and marketing work you will be a far more attractive proposition for them.

Second, you could just adopt some lessons from this book as you go.

If you just can't pause the dream book project you're working on, there are still plenty of lessons in this book you can use to adapt to your current process.

***

My motivation for writing this book is to pay forward the experiences I gained writing my first book.

I'm hoping I can convince you it's not always the best idea to just dive headlong into writing your epic dream book as the first thing you ever do. Write a book to learn how to write a book. Be comfortable making mistakes.

I'm also hoping to make you aware that the rollout of books based on AI is going to make it progressively harder for most first-time authors.

As a new writer, it's never been more important to get moving quickly.

8

You need to get writing. Now!

There's never been a better time to be a first-time author, and there's never been a worse time!

Technologies that help you write, edit, publish, distribute and market your book have never been better, cheaper and easier to use.

But there's a threat looming on the horizon, and the threat is probably closer than you think.

That threat is AI.

Right now it's absolutely possible to write a book, fact or fiction, on a subject that you have absolutely no idea about.

I could have written this book, in half the time, using Chat GPT to fill out the chapters for me. I chose not to.

Many others are less scrupulous.

If you look at Reddit and listen to podcasts on self-publishing (and even traditional publishing) you'll hear "author-preneurs" openly bragging about how they are using these technologies to spew out a multitude of books, so they can leverage the online sales algorithms to make money.

These aren't rogue individuals. They're highly geared and resourced companies with massive teams of cheap, pay-by-the-hour writers who don't give a damn about what they're creating. They have no moral compass, it's all about the fast money.

Non-Fiction and picture-based books are most at risk because they are easy to scrape and replicate using AI.

You can be assured that AI's ability to create fiction will advance in leaps and bounds, as AI scrapes words and images from books, just like yours, to create new content for the charlatans.

As a new author, time is an issue for you. Right now.

Currently, you are competing with other new authors. Real humans who are genuinely writing original books.

Soon you will be competing with a multitude of literary sausage factories who will turn out books based on what big data is telling them about market trends. These sausage factories will include grey divisions sprouted by the reputable publishing players in the current market.

Your ability to market your book will also suffer. Soon you'll be competing with expert teams of online marketers with superior tools, resources and money.

The imperative has never been more urgent to get your book out.

Sooner rather than later.

***

Now you understand the imperative to get moving, lets dive into the common mistakes most new writers make with their first book, based on my recent experiences.

9

Mistake #1

Not Finding Your Creative Time And Space.

In an ideal world, when writing a book, you'd isolate yourself in a log cabin in the woods and not come out until you've completed your perfect manuscript.

Ta Dah! It's done, and it's perfect!
No distractions.
No unexpected family problems.
No work emergencies to deal with.

Of course, you'd have a kitchen that would magically restock itself with meals, munchies and coffee.
I don't know about you. I don't live in that world.

We all have to contend with our daily lives. With constant distractions from family, friends, and work. You'll fall ill. Work will flare up. The wheels will fall off things and force you to change your schedule at the last minute. If you want to write effectively, in amongst all of this rampant mayhem, you need to find your "creative space".

Your creative space isn't just a physical room with a computer, table, and a chair. It's a combination of several things: First, it's about the writing process you adopt to make sure you give your story the best chance to flow out of your body, through your fingers, and onto the computer screen. Second, it's about the physical space you choose to sit down in front of a screen and write. Third, it's also about how you organise your calendar to fit your writing into your busy week.

Let's look at these individually.

Your writing process.

Let's assume you won't be writing your first book by locking yourself up in a log cabin in the woods for a few months. Like most of us, you'll be trying to fit it into the nooks and crannies of your normal life.

For decades now, we've been told that we need to multi-task if we want to "get ahead" in life. "You need to be able to pat your head and rub your tummy at the same time".

That's probably good advice for managing your career or your family, but it's definitely not good for writing.

Multi-tasking kills your ability to write.

The biggest mistake new authors make is to assume you can just slide the process into the gaps in your everyday life. Your writing sessions get jammed haphazardly amongst the nooks and crannies.

It feels effective, but it's incredibly inefficient. It slows you down massively.

I was listening to a podcast recently where a psychologist was talking about the impact of multi-tasking on your ability to get a task done. He'd conducted a study where they asked groups of people to complete IQ tests.

One half of the people in the study were sozzled. They drank a lot of alcohol before they did the test.

The other half were perfectly sober, but someone was distracting them occasionally while they were trying to complete the test. They had to multi-task.

The result was surprising.
The drunk people scored much higher than the multi-taskers.

In their book, The Power of Full Engagement, James Loehr and Tony Schwartz suggest "you need twenty-five minutes to get fully up to speed on anything. Opposing that is the fact that on average we get interrupted every 11 minutes. If you're interrupted that carefully built mental architecture collapses. It can take hours of work just to get back to the same state of awareness." That's the price you pay.

There are many ways multi-tasking kills your creative process.

- Every time you switch between tasks, your brain takes time to refocus. This causes delays and reduces your overall efficiency. Studies have shown that multi-tasking can lead to longer completion times compared to focusing on doing one task at a time.

- Switching between tasks can overload your working memory, which holds and processes your chapters, acts, character traits and your overall story. It's like running a computer with very little RAM. All your software just slows down as it struggles to get multiple things done.

- Distractions restrict your brain's capacity for reflection and deep thinking. In writing a book, the creative solutions you need to develop often require uninterrupted focus and space for ideation, which is disrupted by multi-tasking. This is important when you are trying to remember the macro aspects like story flow, pacing and character development while you are writing the nitty-gritty of the sentences in paragraphs of your book at the same time.

- Dealing with new, or even impending, distractions can lead to rushed or incomplete writing sessions. That haste can lead to lower-quality writing results.

For a solid creative process, you really need to keep the level of multi-tasking to a minimum.

Your physical writing space.

The place you sit down to write is really hard to control. It depends totally on your lifestyle and living conditions. For a lucky few, it will be a dedicated room. For many, it will be a busy corner of a noisy breakfast table.

No matter what your writing space looks like, there are two factors that will decide how well it works.

First, it needs to be as free of distraction as possible.

Second, you need to set it up easily when you start, and pack it up just as easily when you finish.

When you get distracted from your writing, the creative process doesn't just pause for a moment, then begin again. When you get distracted, your creative process actually goes backwards.

If you stop to answer an email notification, it takes your head out of the storyline you are writing.

If someone comes into your space and asks you a question, you might end up getting pulled away to do something for them.

Every distraction pulls your head out of the story-world you are living in while you are writing. It takes time to get your head back into that world each time you return to your writing. More about this in Chapter 11.

If it's too busy, think about getting out.

If your day-to-day writing space is too distracting, consider getting out of it.

The easiest way to find a quiet writing space is to head to a local library.

If there isn't a library nearby, you can always find a local cafe that will be happy for you to sit there for hours, and use their Wi-Fi, in return for being a regular customer. Have a quick chat with the store manager first to make sure they're cool with the idea.

Think outside the square. I once wrote a screenplay by getting a friendly neighbour to let me have access to their empty house each day after they left for work. I just wandered around there after 9:00 a.m. and let myself in. It was bliss. She adored the idea that a movie was being written on her kitchen table while she was at work.

How you calendar your regular writing sessions.

Your regular writing time needs to become a non-negotiable part of your weekly schedule.

My simple solution (which was an idea I stole from a podcast) was to treat my writing time like I would treat a doctor's appointment. It's important, and it's not movable. Put your writing time into your calendar like it's a regular appointment. A really important one!

Ideally, try to write in the same place whenever you sit down in front of the keyboard. You need to build a mental connection that when you are in that space; you are there to write, and only to write.

Scheduling a regular writing time isn't easy.

I've tried every way to schedule my writing time. Mornings. Evenings. Burst days. Intensive weekends. Locking myself away for a few days.

Surprisingly, I've ended up being an early morning writer. I would never have guessed this when I started. I've never been a morning sort of person. Now I find if I get up really early in the morning I can get a lot of writing done, and still find that I have most of the day left to do my other daily activities. I get breakfast and other stuff out of the way before I start, so I'm not tempted to have a break in the middle of it all.

I hated writing in the morning at first, but I've learned to love it. It's been a bit like finding time to go to the gym.

Maybe humans are wired that way. Over time, you just learn to adapt to new ways of doing things, like you build stronger muscles.

I wasn't a morning person, but I forced myself to become one, and now I see the benefits of it.

Tell people what you are doing.

The other important thing you need to do is to tell your family and friends what you are doing with your writing time and place. If you make sure they are clear about the times that you are planning to carve out, they will be less likely to distract and annoy you during those times.

I've gathered some tips on the following pages to minimise the impact of multi-tasking and distractions on your writing.

Set some goals.

You need to set some goals, but that doesn't mean how many words you've written.

I must admit, I'm not a big fan of setting a word count per session or day as a goal. I've tried that and it leads to a situation where you're just trying to pump out as many words as possible, while not really giving a damn about the quality of the writing or how it adds to the storyline. I like to review the amount of words I've written at the end of the session just to get a feeling of "achievement", but I never try to treat it as something that shows success.

My primary goal in every writing session is to advance the story.

I think of my writing goals in terms of reaching a significant point in a character arc, or completing a particular plot point before I finish my session. It doesn't really matter how many words I've written or how long it took.

For example, in my book Weed War, there are several fight scenes between the drug cartel thugs and the characters in the book. So my aim would be to do something like complete a fight scene between two people during a writing session. That way, when I started the next writing session, I had a very clear starting point and didn't have to waste a lot of time reviewing where I was at.

Know when you are done.

If you feel you've lost your momentum, then get out of the creative space and take a break. If you have allocated three hours for a writing session and you find that two hours in you've run out of puff, don't just sit there trying to force yourself to write something. Get out of the space for 15 minutes, then try and start afresh.

Try to keep the activities during your quick break fairly mindless. Don't do something that's mentally stimulating. Have a coffee. Go for a walk. Feed the dog. Go for a drive. Have a shower. Then try getting back into it for another sprint.

Don't sit down and try to answer your emails for the day or plan your next holiday. Processes like that will drag your head completely out of the story you were working on.

Your aim should be to just reset mentally.

Make your environment as distraction-free as possible.

You need to think about your potential distractions in two ways; on the screen and off the screen.

On the screen.

Don't leave windows open while you write that could distract you. Never leave email, notifications or messaging open in case something comes in.

Off the screen.

Try to pick a room where people won't be entering or moving around while you are writing. Consider using noise cancelling headphones if you are in a noisy environment. Keep your desk uncluttered, but also make sure that you have easy access to things like drinks and snacks, so you don't have to get up and leave the space if you get thirsty or hungry.

Get technically organised.

If you are just writing in Microsoft Word, at least the investigate some software options that can help minimise your clutter and keep your writing organised. Watch some YouTube videos about how other authors do it.

My sister has written several books using Word, and she has become a veritable demon in finding ways to use it to reduce clutter.

I use Scrivener to map out and plan complex story lines and characters. It took me a long time to learn it and I actually gave up on it twice during the process. If you're writing a heavily researched book, something like Scrivener is a godsend.

Once I've broken the back of the story in Scrivener, I shift it over to Atticus because it's a much better software tool for formatting the final output of your book and e-book versions.

Make sure you spend some of your writing time researching the best tools for your writing process. I wasted weeks trying to use Scrivener to format the paperback version of my first book. I didn't find out that Scrivener was terrible for formatting until I vented my frustration on a Reddit publishing thread.

I also use the dictation function for most of my core writing, then do my tweaking using the keyboard. There are plenty of free voice-to-text plugins available for web browsers. The function built into Google Docs is amazingly accurate at turning your spoken word text on the screen. I use a web service called speechtexter which is also amazingly accurate.

It takes a bit of practice, but it's a much more efficient way of getting the words out onto the screen in front of you.

The sound of me talking to my computer all the time drives my wife crazy.

Set some boundaries with others.

When you find a place and time where you can focus on your writing, make sure you tell other people what you're doing and how they should interact with you. If others share your writing space, this is important.

You can't blame your family for interrupting you if you haven't made it clear when, and where, you have carved out time for your writing.

10

Mistake #2

Writing Your First Book With A Complex Storyline.

When writing my first book, this was my biggest learning curve

When I started writing Weed War, I was aiming to tell a truly epic story. My story had lots of characters, each of whom had back stories that needed to be built and expanded upon.

The storyline was complex. It switched back and forth in time. From childhood to adulthood. From the past until present day. It shifted locations to keep things interesting.

I'm sure an experienced writer would have handled these time and location slippages with ease. For me, it just ended up in a first draft that was a confusing mess. I just didn't have the skills yet to do it properly.

For your first book, the key is to keep your story simple and linear. Make it as easy as possible to write.

Publish and be damned.

I actually published the first messy, complex draft of my first book.

I was prepared to live with the story-telling mistakes I'd made. My priority was to move rapidly on to my second book. I also have to admit that, after the whack-a-mole process of line editing, I was well and truly sick and tired of reading the story repeatedly, looking at grammar and typos.

Then something unexpected happened.

I discovered the publisher had a sixty-day grace period in which you could change the book for free. About thirty days had passed, so time was running out. That motivated me to try something different.

My first thought was that it would be impossible to simplify and streamline the book I'd written. I was sure the story just wouldn't work that way. Tick. Tick. Tick. I only had 3 weeks to do something.

I decided to sacrifice one weekend trying to "reshuffle the deck" of the story. My aim was to see if I could make it simpler and more linear. If I didn't make genuine progress by the end of the weekend, I was just going to leave the book as it was. Warts and all.

Killing your babies.

The first thing I did was axe a whole pile of unimportant characters.

A police officer I had built a full character profile for just became "the cop".

A bunch of mercenary bikies and soldiers that featured in the main action sequences of the book just became "thugs" (rather than named and identified characters). I got rid of entire chapters to take away characters arcs that didn't drive the story forward.

I killed fifty pages of the book. The story was far less complex.

The next thing I did was reshuffle the chapters to tell the story in a linear way, rather than switching backwards and forwards in time.

The story still seemed to hold together, so I spent a lot of time over the following two weeks wildly knitting the chapters back together again.

Over the course of three weeks, I rewrote the book.

The result surprised me.

What began as "mission impossible" ended up as a massive improvement to the original story. Best thing I ever did!

This was a massive learning. It reminded me of one of the old sayings in writing advertising copy: "You have to learn to kill your babies". This means editing out something you love in order to make the story better.

The lessons I learned while killing some babies in my first book have put me in a brilliant position as I move on to drafting my epic bushranger novel. The three weeks of writing madness paid off in unexpected ways.

The irony.

My motivation stemmed from the discovery of the publisher's sixty-day grace period for free changes.

That motivation led to three weeks of torrid writing to see if I could make the story work in a more linear format.

Two days before the deadline passed, I replaced the content of the book. I was immensely happy with what I'd done.

I never even thought about how much it would cost me to make changes AFTER the deadline expired. I later discovered the cost of replacing the text inside the book, after the deadline, was just $50.

Best $50 I ever saved.

In summary, my advice for the storyline of your first book is:

- Accept that, with your first book, you aren't an experienced writer yet.

- Keep your story simple and linear, so it's much easier to write.

- Don't overload the story with lots of character development and arcs. Keep the focus on your main characters.

- Learn to kill your babies.

These will all put you in much better shape when you move forward to write your epic dream book.

II

Mistake #3

Shooting For Perfection.

Most writers want the first draft of their manuscript to be perfect. To be the absolute best reflection of what they can do.

This means they labour and toil for weeks and months and years, even decades, to get a perfect story down onto paper. Many just lose their love for the process along the way and give up.

> Twenty years from now, you will be more disappointed by the things that you didn't do than by the ones you did do. So throw off the bowlines. Sail away from the safe harbour. Catch the trade winds in your sails. Explore. Dream. Discover.' - Mark Twain

I love this quote from Mark Twain, especially the part about sailing away from safe harbours.

The traditional publishing industry seems to have a "rule book" that every author, including you, needs to follow slavishly. That rule book wants stamp out "mistakes", whether that be story structure, format, character development or just plain old typographical errors.

So, we aim for perfection, trying to follow every rule and industry norm. Unfortunately, this means that many significant stories never see the light of day.

Like Mark Twain, I believe it's good to "throw off the bowlines" and risk making mistakes. That's how you really learn to write. It's how you find your voice. It lets you move fast.

To quote the Duke of Wellington, sometimes you have to bite the bullet and "publish and be damned".

"If it ain't on the page, it ain't on the stage."

This is an adage in the screenwriting business.

It laments that, for every finished screenplay that gets pitched to Hollywood, there are thousands of others that lay, incomplete, on people's computers and will probably never see the light of day. They remain unfinished. The writers never got to a point where they thought it was ready to show to someone. Then they just lost interest in it.

Even if you are just writing for passion, you need to set a timeline to finish.

I realized this when I was writing a screenplay on a famous Australian explorer. People had documented his life extensively. It was an epic story.

My ears pricked up when I listened to an interview on the radio one morning. The guest was one of the explorer's granddaughters. She'd inherited access to all of his old archives and paperwork. A treasure trove of source material. I think she must have been about 90 years old.

She told the interviewer how she had spent the last 12 years meticulously assembling all the materials and writing them into his biographical story. As the interview continued, it became apparent that, although she had invested over a decade of time, she was still a long way from getting a manuscript completed and ready to give to a publisher.

The interview deeply saddened me because I distinctly felt her epic story would never be published.

Write a book to learn how to write a book.

The first book that you write doesn't have to be your epic novel.

That's why I decided the focus of my first book wouldn't be the epic Australian bushranger story I was originally burning to tell. Many authors I've met have spent many years drafting their first manuscript. I got a strong feeling that some of them will never finish.

I didn't want to do it that way.

Rather than trying to conceive, and then birth, a big epic story from the get-go, I set myself a rigid six-month time frame to write something shorter. Something with an easier topic.

I was prepared to live with all mistakes I made along this "temporary" author's journey of discovery. Then I'd move on to write my big kahuna.

***

Don't get me wrong here.

Aiming for perfection with your first book is a great idea if you are only writing for passion. Sales be damned!

If you're writing for a paying career, consider two things;

If you park your dream book for a moment, and write a short, easy one instead, the experience you gain will dramatically improve your dream book when you write it.

If you write, publish, market and sell a short, easy book, you will learn a lot about the publishing industry and how it works. This will pay dividends when you sit down to write your dream book (and when you approach traditional publishers with the manuscript).

12

Mistake #4

Not Understanding Editing and Formatting Before You Write.

This chapter looks at three aspects of editing and formatting a first-time writer needs to be aware of:

First, maintaining your momentum.
Second, the need to understand the five main types of editing.
Third, an understanding that making mistakes isn't a bad thing.

Momentum. 'Make it exist, then make it good'.

In the last chapter we talked about how the worst thing you can do when you're writing your first book is to meticulously wordsmith (and then re-wordsmith) everything as you are writing.

Maintaining momentum is key.

You need to craft a great story (make it exist), then you can focus on editing and formatting (make it good).

The process of constantly word-smithing and reworking specific narrative and dialogue just fractures your writing process. You need to build and maintain momentum, forcing everything out of your brain, through your fingertips and onto your computer screen.

I do this by writing a first draft that is really just a long list of bullet-pointed action sequences. I try to give little thought to narrative, dialogue or character building. It's literally a long list of points saying:

- This happens...

- And then that happens...

- And then another thing happens...

- Then the character's world blows up because this happens...

- They get back on the right path by doing this...

- Another obstacle comes up when this happens...

The first version of the story that ends up in Scrivener is just a list of sentences describing what happens from the start to the end of the story.

I typically use the "clothesline method" to maintain some sort of structure. I also use Aaron Sorkin's "Intention and Obstacle" approach to story building (Someone wants something. Something stands in their way of getting it). You can simply Google both to find out more.

The last thing I'm thinking about is grammar and prose. I'm trying to move fast rather than be perfect.

When I reach the end of this process, I have a crude format of the story, but it gives me an incredible amount of flexibility to move things around to make the story better.

Eventually I'll reach a point where I'll think, *'I like how this story and structure is working'*.

Then I move on to expand the story out with dialogue, narrative and action.

Some developmental editing is handy during the early stages of writing your first draft, but you should really try to avoid getting bogged down in the finicky aspects of editing and formatting just to make the manuscript look good on paper.

The five main types of editing?

I'm going to spend some time in this chapter explaining how the editing process works. From end to end. Mainly because I didn't really understand much about it before I started. Editing breaks down into five classic stages.

1. **Developmental Editing**
2. **Line Editing**
3. **Copy Editing**
4. **Proofreading**
5. **Fact Checking**

Let's look at how this works for your first book.

1: Developmental Editing.

This is where you get someone to look at the overall structure and content of your first draft, considering things like plot character development, pacing and tone. It's like taking a helicopter view of your story. You can do this while writing your first draft or after you finish it.

You can hire a paid professional as your development editor. For my first book, it was my wife, who is an avid reader. She burns through an amazing amount of books each year. I trust her opinion implicitly.

Be careful who you select to do it.

I've listened to a lot of podcasts on this topic. Most authors go through a few developmental editors before they find the one that they are comfortable with. So don't assume that the first one you use will be the best.

If, like me, you go down the "family and friends" path, be very careful about who you select.

I read a great story online about a guy who was getting his father to review his science fiction story. He hated the feedback. It was really negative. Then his brother reminded him that their father hated Star Wars and wasn't really into science fiction at all.

Don't just throw a finished draft at them.

During the really early stages, I often found it beneficial to just verbally talk someone through the story. Over, say, ten minutes, so it wasn't a drag.

All I was trying to discover was which parts excited, confused or bored them. This was always much more efficient than giving them a thick print-out and asking them to go away and read it.

Accept that you are an inexperienced writer.

If I gave you a saw, some nails and some timber, I wouldn't expect you to immediately be able to build a house.

It's the same with writing. Even if you are incredibly gifted, you still have to go through a learning curve.

The main thing to keep in mind is, at this point in your writing journey, it's a good thing to make mistakes. Who cares if you accidentally create holes in your plot, or if you screw up the timeline? It's not a crime to be inconsistent about characters and locations. The process of repairing these errors will be incredibly valuable when you eventually write your dream book.

The single most important thing I kept in mind when writing my first book was that I was an inexperienced author.

In my first book, I made two major mistakes. Later I had to pick them apart and rebuild the story. It was painful.

The first was that my original storyline shifted around in time a lot. It often went back and forth between the past, the future, and the current day. I did it that way because I didn't think the story could be told in any other way.

After finishing the first outline, and getting some feedback from people that had read it, I realised that it just created a level of confusion. I had a big problem because I thought it would be impossible to write the story in a purely linear format (so the times and places were easier to keep track of).

I'd convinced myself that it was a mistake I would just have to live with.

I was wrong.

The second was that I wrote the book in US English rather than my native British English.

My logic was that America would be the biggest market for a book like this. Writing it in US English would make it easier to read. In retrospect, this actually made no sense because it was an Australian story, set in Australia, with Australian characters.

Stupid me.

It led to weeks of frustration in the editing process. I won't make that mistake again in my next book.

2: Line Editing.

This level of editing looks at your writing from a paragraph and sentence level and also considers the writing style. Once again, my main learning was that this step takes a lot longer than you think it will, even if you slavishly word-smithed as you were writing.

From what I've read online, many authors like to use the Read Aloud function in Word to help with this stage of the editing.

3: Copy Editing.

I call this the whack-a-mole stage.

This is where you focus on things like grammar, punctuation, syntax, and spelling. You'll also look at formatting issues like headings, paragraphing and numerical styles.

Copy editing will take longer than you think.

When I finish my first draft, I thought the line and copy editing stage might take a few days. Maximum a week.

It ended up taking months. If you've got unlimited time and unlimited money, pay someone to do this for you.

By the time I finished copy editing my first book, I hated it and never wanted to pick it up again. It was gruelling.

That said, the frustrating process I went through bought a lot of rigour to my future writing.

I would also strongly recommend looking at writing tools like ProWritingAid (PWA) to continuously pick up simple copy errors why you are writing your first draft. It will save you a massive amount of time (and aggravation) later on. Find out more at my author's website if you are interested.

4: Proofreading.

In my first book, I fretted a lot about this. I was adamant that the book would go out with zero mistakes and typos in it.

Once again, if you have unlimited time and money, pay someone to do your proofreading. If, like most of us, you can't afford to do it that way, you need to learn to take a chill pill.

You aren't going to be sent to jail if you publish a book with the couple of innocent mistakes in it. If it's a good story, people aren't going to shit-can your book online because it had five words spelled wrong out of the 80,000 you wrote.

Since going through the painful proofreading process on my first book, I can't believe the number of typos and mistakes that I now pick up in books by major authors and in things like newspaper and magazine stories.

The final version of Weed War that went out had two typos in it. Strangely enough, I told people about it and challenged them to find the mistakes. Nobody ever could. One mistake was on the third page. I could see them physically reading the chapter and not clocking the blatant typo that was in it.

5: Fact Checking.

This is an important step if your book is based on facts rather than fiction.

My simple advice here would be to pick a topic, or a way of broaching that topic, that minimises the risks involved in fact checking.

Change your mindset to "It's OK to make mistakes".

I like mistakes.

Just as with cooking, sometimes a mistaken ingredient can cause something wonderful. My wife won't cook anything without a recipe. That's her style. I'm the opposite. I love grabbing a bunch of ingredients and seeing what I can create with them. Sometimes the results are terrible, but sometimes they're great.

My biggest issue with an overreliance on professional editors is that they can harm your unique writers "voice".

A great example of this is Peter Carey's epic and multi award-winning book called the True history of the Kelly gang. It's a story about the famous bushranger Ned Kelly, but is told in the format of a group of written packages he left behind that talked about his life.

The book breaks every single rule of format and editing, but, at the same time, it's brilliant and compelling.

If you find a mistake in this book, it will bring a smile to my face.

Another risk with paid editing is what I call "Star Wars (or Marvel) Syndrome". Professional editors want to make sure that your book is "successful". That's good, but sometimes that means they want you to write your book in a "certain way" to appeal to publishing industry norms, or structure and write it in a way proven successful for your book type in the past. It's the reason that the Star Wars movie franchise has become bland and formulaic. Everyone wants to just repeat the winning story formula.

This formulaic approach means that most books in genres blur together because they're all forced into the same set of rules.

An editor might tell a writer with a "weird" or "risky" style to restructure and rewrite their book completely to meet industry standards.

Sometimes that advice is absolutely correct.

Sometimes it isn't.

Some tips for ebook formatting.

Formatting your book for a printed copy is relatively easy. Most formatting software lets you output a PDF that looks exactly the same as how your final printed version will look. What you see is what you get.

Formatting your ebook is more challenging.

You are going to sell the lion's share of the ebook version of your story to people who will use Kindles or iPads. So you need to make sure it looks as good as possible on both core devices.

Some of the software tools for writing and editing make it incredibly easy to output your e-book version. I use Atticus because the creation of the final eBook file is an easy, streamlined process.

That said, there were also many instances where the final ebook formatting on Kindle and iPad didn't quite match what I was expecting.

For the sake of testing, I didn't have an ebook that I could download from an online bookstore. So I had to find a work-around.

By saving my ebook file on a Google Drive folder I was able to send my ebook version direct to my Kindle (using "Send to Kindle") and my iPad (by downloading it from Google Drive and opening it in Apple Books), this let me see exactly how my book looked on each of those major platforms before I committed to distributing it.

This pre-publishing review process allowed me to make many changes to the e-book version that made it look better on both of those core devices.

Always physically check how it looks on iPad and Kindle before you approve the book to be distributed on global ebook platforms.

Find out more at my author's website if you are interested in up-to-date formatting tips for audio books.

13

Mistake #5

Thinking About Publishing Too Late In Your Process.

When you've written the first draft of your book, you're only a small way along the journey toward finishing it.

Looking back, I wish I'd spent more time learning about the publishing and distribution process back at the beginning. Well before I started typing.

This is for two main reasons:
First, some aspects of the publishing and distribution process might influence how you write your first draft.
Second, I was forced to make my publishing and distribution decisions in a rush, later in the process.

My aim in this chapter is to give you a helicopter view of the decisions you'll need to make once you've written your first draft.

Get a quick helicopter view before you begin.

If you haven't done it already, take some time off from writing your first book and spend it researching your future options in the publishing industry. Particularly, spend some time learning about self-publishing, even if you are only planning to consider traditional publishing.

- Do a Google search for the platforms available for self-publishing. Watch some YouTube videos by authors who have experience with them. Don't do a deep-dive, you just want to get a high level view of what's available to make your paperback, e-book or audiobook a reality.

- As a counterpoint, watch a couple of videos on YouTube where authors talk about their experience getting a newbie manuscript in front of a traditional publisher.

- Then Google a list of the options to distribute your book (Amazon, Apple, bookstores, markets, etc). Get a broad understanding of the sales channels and the formats you can make your book available in.

After you've done the above, summarise what your gut-feeling is about the best option for you to follow. You can always change your mind later on.

Consider the financial and lifestyle implications.

Your publishing choices will have financial implications, so it's good to understand them early.

Start by watching some YouTube videos and follow some chat groups that talk about how authors are making a living from their books. Get a feeling about how other authors decided what they were going to be charging reach version of their book (hardcover, paperback, ebook and audio book) and how much they wanted to make per sale. We'll look at this in more detail in the next chapter.

Armed with that knowledge, spend some time thinking about how the books you write and publish will impact how you choose to live.

Are you writing just for passion? Is it ultimately going to be your full-time income? Is it a side hustle while you continue to do your day job?

Then have a think about what your gut says will be the best type of book for you to tackle for your first effort. Then ask yourself, how hard, or easy, will it be for your type of book to get in front of potential buyers? A gothic Japanese love story is a very different beast to a Chicago murder mystery. The publishing strategies will be very different for each.

Do the numbers.

Jot down some realistic goals you'd need to achieve each year to make the task financially viable.

Find ten books that are like the book you are planning to write and jot down what each of them is selling for right now (paperback, ebook and audiobook versions). Use that information to answer the following questions.

How much income per month do you need to justify the work you will put in?

How many sales per month would you need to make that amount of income?

What will be your income from each book sold (your royalty income, not the book's cover price)

What can you afford to spend on editing, design and other costs?

How much do you need to set aside for tax and other costs?

What sales channels will work best for my book (eg, Kindle Unlimited vs Amazon Books vs Selling at markets and fairs)?

Should I write a single book or a series?

How much can I afford to allocate to marketing (launch phase, then monthly)?

How you are going to tackle the design of your book?

Your cover design and blurb are as critical as the words inside your book. If you screw the cover up, chances are people will never get around to reading what's inside the book.

Your cover design and blurb aren't just about being pretty or striking. The way you approach the design elements and wording has to be very strategic. To do it properly, you either have to allocate some money to get it done professionally or allow extra time for trial and error if you are going to do it yourself.

You don't want to be thinking about book design the day before you are due to upload it to the publishing platform. The design of your cover isn't a decision you want to make hastily.

The same goes for the size of the book you choose. I chose a larger 9x6 format for my first book because I thought the target reader group would be older and therefore would appreciate a larger font size to make it easy to read.

You also need to allow some trial and error to see how your book will look in electronic formats like Kindle and iPad.

I created some graphics for my first book that looked fantastic against a light-colored eBook reader background. Through trial and error, I discovered they looked terrible if the page colour was set to black for nighttime reading. I had to remake all the graphics at the last minute to make sure they worked with both dark and light backgrounds.

Spend some time learning about meta-data.

When people are searching for books to buy online, they are typing words into a search bar to find options. When you publish your book, you will need to define the keywords that you want to attach to it to make it as findable as possible during a search.

Try to allocate a few hours one day to watch some videos on how this works. You don't need to become an expert, but you need to be familiar with the concept so you don't end up doing it in a mad rush when your manuscript is complete and ready to publish.

One thing that I hadn't considered when I published my first book was what the subtitle of the book would be.

I thought the title on the cover would be the main thing that mattered, but the subtitle appears prominently on just about every online listing. It plays an important role in how effectively your metadata works.

Understand how ISBN's work.

There are many opinions on how essential these are. Most people think there are prerequisite. Some people think they are completely unnecessary. Some people use free options to reduce their costs. I'm no expert on free ISBNs, but everything I've read suggests you should steer clear of them.

One of the best pieces of advice I received about ISBN numbers is that the primary services, like Thorpe-Bowker, offer bundle deals where you can buy ten ISBN numbers for a fairly cheap price. Last time I looked, you could buy ten for $88, versus just one for $44. I've already chewed through most of that initial ten I bought.

Build a foundation for your long-term brand as an author.

The branding of your first book is important.
The branding of you, as an author, is equally important.
No matter how you are going to publish your book, you need to think about the tools you'll need to build your brand as an author. It's an important part of your publishing approach.

When someone looks at your book, in a bookstore, or online, they wonder about what the story will be like.

Equally, they wonder about what you are like as an author. So your own back-story is equally important to the ones you give your characters. It's critical if you are doing non-fiction books where your credibility and chutzpah as an expert are important. So, you should definitely think about creating a simple author website.

I used WordPress to create a really simple website about me and my writing. tonysharples.com

I originally built it with lots of pages, blogs and links but eventually decided that would be too much of a hassle to maintain, so I culled it down to just two simple pages.

The first page just contains:

More blurb about my first book.

An overview of my personal story.

A teaser for my next book.

A really simple form where people can contact me (and I can capture their email details).

The second page of the website contains some sample paragraphs of writing from key parts of the book to give people a flavour for it.

In terms of design, I focused on how it would work on a mobile phone screen. I also put a QR code that links to my author's site on the back cover of my book. This would allow anyone with a mobile phone, standing in a bookshop, to just scan the code and find out all about me and the book. Author sites are a good place to put your juiciest reader reviews.

As I've mentioned earlier, my current priority is writing my second and third books. After an initial rush of enthusiasm, I decided not to expand into social media with things like channels on Facebook and TikTok, a presence on Instagram or a feed on X. All of those will eventually play a role but they aren't right for me at this point in time.

I also went through a lot of back-and-forth signing up for Amazon Author Central. It took weeks. I've found it to be a bit of a waste of time. It seems like they recently removed a lot of the functionality that made it worthwhile as a proxy for your author site.

Wherever possible, you need to capture the details of people who have bought your book or have expressed an interest in it, so you can contact them with news when future books come out.

Most of the new website builders, like WordPress or Wix, come with very simple ways of adding forms for people to sign up for a newsletter.

Start with something really simple. Just a form that sends details to your email address. After you build your eventual library of books for sale, and boost your expertise in marketing, you can grow to a more sophisticated email strategy.

On the subject of email, don't just use your normal everyday email details in your book or on your author's site. Spam is a constant issue and you don't want to risk flooding your everyday email account. I just set up a new Gmail account for my book using sharples.writer@gmail.com. That way I can clearly identify any email that's coming in from my book or my author's site.

14

Mistake #6

Not Understanding The Economics.

I've learned a lot about publishing, profits and marketing during the process of birthing my first book.

It's opened my eyes to a world I never imagined.

It also told me I needed to ask myself a really important question before I even began my writing journey.

Why do I want to be an author?

Writing for passion.

Authors can be strange folk.

When I read about new authors' experiences, I'm always amazed at how many writers are just in it for the passion.

Many writers just don't seem to be interested in the money. They're happy if a few people read their story, despite the massive amount of hours and toil they've put into writing it. If they do the math on their sales, they discover they've really been paying themselves around $1 an hour for all the hard effort they've put in. But their comment is still, 'Meh, that's okay, I'm just happy if someone read it'.

You wouldn't hear a shopkeeper or a business person saying, 'I don't care if I don't make any money. I'm just happy that people came into the shop and looked at the stuff I've got for sale'.

The passion aspect of writing is weird. It's also wonderful.

Many authors feel compelled to tell a story that needs to be told. They'll toil for years, or even decades, to make it perfect. I love that approach to writing.

What I don't love is that many of these epic stories never see the light of day. They end up as a manuscript that's never quite finished. Or become that miserable file always lurking in the background on your computer hard drive, taunting you to complete it one day.

If you write for passion, I doff my hat to you and wish you well. I truly believe you are the lifeblood of the literary world.

Treating it more like a business.

Other writers are more results-oriented.

They might aspire to be the next JK Rowling or Tom Clancy. Maybe they want to write a book that will benefit their business success. At a minimum, they need their book sales to contribute towards their house payments and cost of living. It needs to pay enough money to make the effort that you put in worthwhile, whether it is your sole income stream or a side hustle.

These writers are in it for a career. Ultimately, they want to quit their day job and make enough money to write books full-time. If you fall into this basket, you really need to have a good hard think about the economics of how it's going to work for you personally and financially. The numbers can be grim.

The www.wordsrated.com website suggests:

The good news:
- 300 million self-published books are sold each year.
- The number of self-published books has increased by 264% in the last five years.
- $1.25 billion worth of self-published books are sold each year
- More than 1,000 self-published authors made $100,000 last year from Amazon.

The not-so-good news:
- 90% of self-published books sell less than 100 copies.
- The average self-published book sells 250 copies.
- 20% of self-published authors report making no income from their books.
- The average self-published author makes $1,000 per year from their books.
- The average self-published book sells for $4.16; the authors get 70% of that. ($2.91)
- 20% of self-published authors report making no income from their books.

How do the numbers apply to your writing career?

One of the first things I did when I began my writing journey is I joined a lot of online chat groups about writing and publishing. I wanted to understand how the economics were working for people entering the business. I found this to be eye-opening, to say the least.

Some writers think about writing as passive income.

They enjoy the creative process, and they treat writing like a side hustle. These authors aim to build a library of books they've written, and that will generate a healthy stream of monthly income for them on the side, while they still continue to do their day job. They've thought about the numbers.

It's clear that there is a group who realise that they'll never make a real living from books, but they are happy to live with that reality. Just being published is enough.

If you fall into this group, you really need to have a think about how much money you are going to need to make from book sales each year to achieve your goal of supplementing your income.

There's a second group that doesn't seem to understand the numbers.

Maybe they think they're writing for passion, but I suspect that they just haven't given proper thought to the actual long-term cost of creating and selling a book.

I was reading a post on a chat group on self-publishing the other day where a guy was proudly announcing that "after three years of hard work writing a single book and spending a lot of money marketing it" he had reached sales of 1000 books. This would mean that, at a realistic margin of a few dollars of book, he's made well less than $10,000 for three years of work. Not to mention the amount of money that he's probably spent on advertising and marketing. Hardly something to crow about.

Of course, I have to admire anyone that has sold a thousand books. That's a colossal achievement. Well above the average, but it was clear from the way the post was written that he planned to use book sales as a major source of his income.

My main point here is that you have to think about the amount of personal "effort" you are going to put in versus what you are going to get out. It's just as important as thinking about things like your story line, character development and plot points.

The Economics of Time.

When considering the business side of writing, there's one other thing I've discovered during the process of completing my first book.

It's something I call "the economics of time".

Writing vs Selling.

Most authors will tell you that you really won't get sales and reader momentum until you have several books available. This makes sense. If you've only got one book of available, and someone really enjoyed reading it, you've got nothing else to offer them. On the other hand, if several books are available, your happy reader is likely to buy more quickly.

When you complete your first book, you'll face a dilemma.

Should you spend your time writing a second and third book, or do you focus on selling your first book to give it the best chance possible?

Every minute you spend tending to the success of your first book is a minute you aren't spending writing your second.

Finding the time to run a marketing campaign.

I've spent a lot of time looking at how first-time authors tackle marketing.

There seem to be 3 common schools of thought.

First, many younger authors are what I would call digital natives. They're active on social media and have probably built a decent presence online already. Most importantly, they enjoy doing stuff on social media. They feel at home across things like Facebook, TikTok an Instagram. This group of people will find digital marketing for books straightforward, and even enjoyable.

Second, there's a group that probably see online marketing as a "necessary evil". It's not something they naturally enjoy doing, but they appreciate that they have to do it to promote their book. This group of people probably going to find it quite tough as they go through a steep learning curve about what works and what doesn't.

I think there's also a third group. These are people that are in the necessary evil camp, but should probably give online marketing a miss in order to focus on other things that might be more important. I've seen lots of posts online that show that this last group really struggle, waste money and eventually become dejected.

Marketing your first book is hard.

Chances are, you aren't a social media expert. That means you are definitely going to spend an enormous amount of effort figuring out how it works. Facebook vs Instagram vs TikTok vs everything else. You'll also blow a lot of money during that process on content creation and wasted advertising campaigns. Online selling platforms, like Amazon, will also be a massive part of your success. Once again, you're probably not an expert in online advertising, keywords and understanding about how book-selling algorithms work.

If you are self-publishing using an online platform, you also need to have a deep understanding of things like meta-data and pricing strategies.

None of those essential marketing approaches are easy topics.

Don't forget you can find more specific and updated information about marketing your book by visiting my author's website.

You need to balance your priorities.

After considering my options, I decided to not actively market my first book.

This was for two reasons:

First, I bought into the commonly-held notion that you get limited returns marketing your first book. If someone likes your first book, they have nothing else to buy from you. It's going to be a long wait before you have a second or third book for them to buy. If you've written and published several books, you may also seem like a less risky proposition to a potential book buyer.

Second, as I'll explain in later chapters, I thought it would be more beneficial to spend my precious time going through a process of learning how to create an audiobook, versus spending that time marketing my first paperback and ebook. I will do a small amount of marketing on Amazon for my first book, but nothing significant. My gut feeling is that I'll be in a much stronger position when I have two or three books available, so getting those books out is my priority for now. Then I'll get more serious about marketing.

As time goes by, I'll add updates on my author's site on how I'm evolving my marketing approach and sales strategy.

One thing I'm doing is testing the Publisher Rocket platform to optimise my sales on Amazon. It's still very early days for that. I'll be putting updates on how that's working on my author's site in the future.

In terms of economics, the main thing to remember is that anything you spend on marketing is a cost that eats into your profit. I see a lot of authors online talking about their monthly sales, or what they are charging as their cover price, but the focus always seems to be on the dollars that are coming in. Not many talk about what they are really making after their advertising and selling costs are taken out of the money they're earning.

Being an author is really no different from running a shop or a business. You can't just focus on how much money is coming into the cash register. You have to allow for all of the selling costs (and things like tax, legals and book-keeping) to gauge the actual effect on your way of life.

15

MISTAKE #7

THINKING GETTING FEEDBACK WILL BE EASY.

Once you finish your first draft, you quickly discover it's really hard to get feedback, paid or unpaid.

Most people will enthusiastically offer to take a draft of your manuscript, or an early copy of your printed book, and excitedly promise they'll read it immediately.

Then, crickets. You hear nothing back from them.

There are a couple of reasons for this.

Maybe it turns out that your book isn't quite their cup of tea and they're too embarrassed to let you know. This just leads to awkward silence rather than active feedback. My mother-in-law enthusiastically offered to read my book and give me some feedback. I happily gave her an early copy of Weed War, not even considering that stories about military kill-teams and violent drug cartels were not exactly topics close to her heart.

The more likely reason you won't get feedback is that reading a book is a big task. It's not like flipping through a newspaper or watching a hyped TV show. I gave my book to many people to read and comment on, but I only really got any sort of constructive feedback from three of the readers.

Don't assume getting feedback on the first draft will be a quick process. Plan ahead, so it doesn't unexpectedly blow a massive hole in your timing plan.

Do some research. Find someone you can pay to give you some valuable feedback quickly. If your budget doesn't allow for that, just plan to move forward based on your gut feel.

If you're writing on a shoe-string, you'll face some compromises trying to get feedback at different stages of your writing and publishing process.

I hadn't really given any thought to getting a professional editor involved in my first drafts, so I published my first book, even though my gut told me the story structure wasn't working perfectly.

It was a compromise. Many writers I spoke to said I was bonkers.

My bigger priority was moving onto my second book, so I was happy with the compromise on the first book I wrote. My primary motivation was my absolute commitment to keep moving forward. I wanted to learn as much as I could before I shifted over to writing the dream book I was originally burning to write.

16

Mistake #8

Not Allowing Time And Money For Marketing.

A recent Reddit thread about self-publishing asked people to list the three major pain-points of the entire process.

One of the authors simply responded, 'That's easy. Marketing. Marketing. Marketing.'

Another added, 'I simply hate, loathe, despise, cannot stand marketing. Not getting traction is the single biggest demotivator for my writing. Not a single investment has paid for itself yet.'

Marketing is a totally different skill to writing, so it's very easy for an author to get lost in the intricacies of how it works. It becomes a never-ending learning experience.

If you get picked up by a traditional publisher, they'll make most of the marketing decisions for you.

If you're self publishing, when you finish your first book, you'll discover the writing was actually the easy part. Publishing is technical, but you can work your way through it. Pricing and marketing is another ball game.

Imagine you have your first book available to buy online. Now you face two big decisions:

Should I spend my time and money marketing my new book?

Or should I invest my time in writing my second and third books?

If you're not juggling a day job, and you've got the finances, you could do both. That's not a reality for most people.

Don't make it a last-minute rush.

I highly recommend that you take a "time out" during the writing process and allocate some mornings to thinking about how you will eventually tackle marketing. Both in terms of the dollars you have to spend and the time you can allocate. Watch some YouTube videos. Scroll through Reddit.

You don't want to be making your marketing decisions in a rush once your book is available for sale.

Do some real-world trial and error.

My gut feel is you can't become an effective marketer by just studying it in advance.

Definitely spend some time researching the options and following social media to see what's working for other authors, but you'll get a better feel for what works, and what doesn't, by testing some marketing campaigns once you have a real book in the marketplace. Then you can really gauge which activities lead to real sales.

Set your priorities.

I decided to focus on writing my second and third books.

I'll only do marketing for my first book if I somehow end up with some spare time to test some options available.

I have put some basics in place. I created an author's website to let people get information about my first book and my future books. It also lets me start to build a mailing list. I took a subscription to Publisher Rocket to make sure that I was really optimising my keyword selection.

The only other thing I've done is allocate some time to learn how to "create an audiobook, by writing an audiobook." My research tells me that's the best source of profitable revenue in my market for my next book.

More about this in Chapter 19.

17

Mistake #9

Not Setting Some Hard Deadlines.

'A goal is a dream with a deadline.' Napoleon Hill

How important is time for you?

If you're writing for passion, the <u>time</u> you take to write your first book isn't so important. The <u>result</u> is important.

If you're writing to eventually create a library of books that will provide a livable income, time is of the essence.

Deadlines refine your thinking.

Time is important.

Deadlines are more important, for many reasons:
- Deadlines keep you focussed and motivated. You progress steadily rather than potter around.

- Just like regular exercise, writing consistently tends to build a stronger writing habit.

There's nothing like an approaching deadline to kill procrastination, or wasting time endlessly trying to perfect your narrative, dialogue and action. An approaching deadline can also force you to consider creative options you might not normally consider.

- Setting a group of manageable milestones (like completing a chapter, rounding out a character arc or finishing a plot point) can make the overall writing tasks seem less overwhelming.

- For a first-time author, deadlines prepare you for what the real world is going to be like once you have several books on the market. Your ability to work to deadlines builds your credibility with editors, agents and collaborators in the future.

Set yourself a ridiculous timing plan.

When I set out to write my first book, I set myself a target of six months to get it done. Having never written a book before, that seemed impossible. I decided, if I missed that timing, I was prepared to walk away from being an author, happy that I had given it a really good shake.

The reason I set this hard deadline is that my research suggested I would eventually need to be capable of writing more than one book a year, if it was going to work financially for me. My goal was that I was going to need to write about twenty books over the next ten years.

This meant I needed to develop an approach to writing that was systematic rather than long-winded.

To be honest, I also knew that the book-police weren't going to come around and drag me off to jail if my six-month deadline blew out to eight months. What did I have to lose?

My current target is to hone my skill, and my process, to a point where I can eventually do three books a year. That's a tall order for anyone.

My secret sauce for sticking to deadlines comes from a simple thought I heard in a podcast on project management for writers.

You should treat your writing time like it was a doctor's appointment. Most people won't shift the doctor's appointment unless a truly dire situation arises. You also put a doctor's appointment into your diary and you shift other things around it.

Of course, a doctor's appointment can be cancelled, but you are going to think long and hard about it.

Take no prisoners.

I also have a bit of a "take no prisoners" approach to meeting my deadlines.

When I did the major redraft of my first book, I gave myself just three weeks. If I didn't achieve something significant, I was 100% prepared to leave the book as it was.

Looking back, setting that lunatic deadline was the best thing I ever did.

The sheer pressure of the deadline eventually forced me to "kill my babies" and make drastic changes to the way the story was told. I eventually took out fifty pages of a story that I had carefully crafted and grown to love. Characters I'd spent weeks developing just disappeared off the page.

I don't think I could have achieved that if I hadn't set a ridiculously hard deadline to get it done.

***

A closing piece of irony.

> 'You don't plan life, it just happens. And you sure as hell can't control the things that happen to you. They just do.'
> – Ines Vieira

It took me six months to write and publish my first book. I met my deadline, technically speaking.

The real story is that my first book took two separate bursts of three-months, with a forced gap in the middle.

I attacked the first three months of writing at my computer with so much vigour I aggravated an old pinched nerve that I had in my neck. I ended up in so much pain that I could no longer write. I had to spend six months doing intensive physio-therapy, eating pain medication like candy and getting lots of cortisone shots.

After six months, it settled down and I could get back into it again.

I just set the clock ticking again on the original six-month deadline.

My advice here is that deadlines are critical to maintaining the momentum of your progress, but you need to manage that momentum in a way that doesn't damage your health, family or work life.

18

Stop Calling Yourself An Author.

If I could give one piece of advice to a first-time writer, it would be to stop calling yourself a writer or an author.

The act of writing is only a small part of the process of giving birth to a book.

You should refer to yourself as a publisher.

You start by writing words, then you take those words and turn them into a format people can read. You might self-publish, or use a traditional publisher, but your primary purpose in life is to get those words into a format that people can see on a page or listen to.

A brilliantly told story that just sits on a computer hard drive forever doesn't do justice to the brilliance of that story. You need to publish it so people can experience it.

Be a publisher, not an author.

19

WHAT SHOULD YOU DO NEXT?

In this chapter, we'll look at how you can go about "writing a book to learn how to write a book".

If you can see the benefit of climbing a small mountain before you tackle your dream book, there are some simple steps to follow.

- Pick a story topic you will find really easy to write about.

- Set yourself a drop-dead timeline to get the book written, published and distributed online. The whole nine yards until you have a book available for sale in the real world.

- Find your creative space and build a consistent writing habit. Minimise multitasking.

- Write a first draft that is simple and linear. Reduce the characters.

- Set aside some time-out sessions to study the industry. Don't deep-dive.

How to find an easy topic for your story.

The best source is going to be something that's directly related to your personal or work experience. It could be about something you find fascinating.

- If you're an accountant, write a fiction book that is set in the world of accounting.

- If you're a volunteer firefighter, write a guide about how to protect your home from a bushfire.

- If you do quilting, write a story about a quilting group.

- If you're a student, write a campus drama or comedy.

- If you're from Macedonia, write a simple Macedonian cookbook or a local folklore tale.

- Write a short story about an interesting chapter of your life.

- Write about the exploits of your mad grandfather.

- Like a classic Indy film, tell a story that happens in one day or in one simple location. A murderous cabin in the woods. Friends gather to mourn a death. A weekend trip that spirals out of control.

Why I chose cannabis, the military, and the drug trade?

My choice was driven by two factors:

First, I wanted to write about a topic that was really engaging.

I knew I wanted to write an adventure fiction novel, so I started thinking about topics that would have lots of scope for action scenes. Drugs and military skirmishes both fit that bill. For my book Weed War, I kept the premise really simple. "What would happen if we woke up one day and the entire global cannabis crop had died?"

My second reason was more personally motivating. I wanted to find a way to involve my son in the writing process. Instead of going on a hike or camping, we would spend some time creating a book together.

He's a bit of a military freak. So I decided I would write a military adventure book. Purely to give me an excuse to use him as my "guide" to how the CIA/Seal Team world thinks and works. I knew his involvement would keep me motivated and wanting to write.

20

A Real World Example.

If you want a good example of how the *"write a book to learn how to write a book"* process works, you're holding it right in your hands, or looking at it on your Kindle screen, or maybe even listening to it as an audiobook.

When I wrote my first the book (Weed War) I was very keen to get it out in every format. Physical, ebook and Audiobook.

My use of IngramSpark (for publishing) and Atticus (for writing and formatting) made the first two of those formats incredibly easy. No problemo.

But an audiobook version seemed like a bridge too far for me.

My first book had too many characters, locations and action scenes to make it an affordable process, particularly given I was probably going to make a lot of mistakes along the way. It would be a gigantic time-suck as well.

I had to make a hard choice.

Navigating my way through the audiobook process as a newbie would have added a lot of time to my schedule. While I was learning the ropes to do that audio-book version, it would mean that I wasn't moving forward on my next main writing project (my epic Bushranger story). A classic Catch-22!

It led me to write this book instead.

I decided to climb an incredibly small mountain. *I'd write an audiobook, in order to learn how to write, publish and market an audiobook.*

Here's how I approached it.

I based it on a topic I could easily write about.

I'd just finished and published my first book, so the entire process was very fresh in mind. I also had some strong opinions about what I had learned, so I chose to write a short book about my experiences.

I purposely kept the number of pages as short as possible.

Surprisingly, keeping the number of pages down was harder than it looked.

My original target was somewhere around eighteen pages. That's IngramSpark's minimum number of pages. The topic kept wanting to expand out to tens of thousands of words. It was a constant battle to keep the word count down. My line in the sand eventually became 100 pages, to keep the book skinny.

To quote Mark Twain; "I apologize for such a long letter - I didn't have time to write a short one"

I set very hard deadlines for the editing process.

The shortness of the book, and the lack of a plot, made this easier. The shortness also made it very easy for me to cajole people to read it and give me feedback quickly.

I published the physical and e-book on IngramSpark

This was easy because I already fully understood the process from my first book. I had become familiar with Atticus, which allowed me to do a fair bit of the basic editing as I was writing. ProWritingAid also helped.

I didn't use a formal book editor because it would have slowed down the process too much.

Finally, I used Generative AI in Photoshop to develop the main cover drawings, for the sake of speed. It let me quickly create the cover artwork. I went for a plain, childish look to make it feel simple to read.

I took a three-week hiatus.

That's right. I wrote, edited and published this book in around 20 working days. I didn't skimp on the content, I just stuck to the rigid timeline I had set, then paced the stages accordingly. This forced me to keep it short and sweet. For the sake of brevity, I was forced to kill lots of my babies along the way.

I've allowed one further week to record the audiobook narrative and prepare the files to upload to an audiobook platform. The book is around 20,000 words, which equates to a two-hour audiobook. Short but sweet.

I made it very clear to my family what I was doing, so they understood my crazy three week schedule.

I'm going to focus the marketing solely on Amazon ads.

This approach focuses on using keywords to make ads pop up beside searches for books on Amazon. That will be much easier to manage than trying to do a multi-channel approach, including things like Facebook, TikTok and YouTube or Google search. And you only pay when someone clicks through.

In summary, I'm writing this book primarily to learn how to create an audiobook - in a manageable way.

This book is short. That will make the audiobook creation task easier and faster.

I've calculated that the audiobook version will be just over two hours long. This means that it will be cheaper and easier to record and I'll also be able to charge a competitive price for it. Any money I make from the paperback and ebook versions will be a bonus.

It's non-fiction, so it's an easier story to tell as an audiobook narrator. It doesn't have the complexity of characters and plot lines that require special reading skills.

Along the way, I'll learn how the audiobook publishing system works. My initial understanding is that it's harder (for tax reasons) if you are based outside of America. In Australia, where I live, I have to find a middleman to handle it for me. I'm planning to use Findaway Voices, which is owned by Spotify, to handle the publishing of the audiobook version (they can push it out to Audible, Apple and Google for me). I'm assuming that will probably eat into my profit margin.

I'll use the knowledge I gain during this creative process to influence how I write my epic Bushranger novel, so it lends itself more easily to an audiobook format when I finally publish it.

This quick trek, on a very small mountain, will really help me conquer the really big one ahead.

I'll add some additional insights about the audiobook process on my author's website.

21

Please Leave A Review.

Reviews are the lifeblood of book marketing.

If you like this book and what it talks about, I'd be incredibly grateful if you could leave a review of it on the site you bought it from.

If you believe it's terrible, I equally appreciate the feedback.

You can also send a review directly via my website www.tonysharples.com

Send your comments by using the email form at the bottom of the homepage.

Links to resources.

For the sake of flexibility, I've created a link to some resources you might find useful as a first-time author.

It is on my author's website at www.tonysharples.com

I put it there so I can update it with new links that I come across and delete any that become dated.

Please feel free to use the email form on the pages of the site to email me any links you think would be worthwhile adding.

As I was about to push the button to publish this book, I stumbled across a quote by George R.R. Martin, author of A Song of Ice and Fire (which became Game of Thrones).

I thought it might be an appropriate way to end.

'One has to start with years of practice with shorter stories until "climbing" Mt. Everest.'   - George R.R. Martin.

www.ingramcontent.com/pod-product-compliance
Lightning Source LLC
Chambersburg PA
CBHW011550070526
44585CB00023B/2533